HOUGHTON MIFFLIN HARCOURT

JOURNEYS

Program Authors

James F. Baumann · David J. Chard · Jamal Cooks
J. David Cooper · Russell Gersten · Marjorie Lipson
Lesley Mandel Morrow · John J. Pikulski · Héctor H. Rivera
Mabel Rivera · Shane Templeton · Sheila W. Valencia
Catherine Valentino · MaryEllen Vogt

Consulting Author
Irene Fountas

 HOUGHTON MIFFLIN HARCOURT
School Publishers

Cover illustration by Jimmy Pickering.

Printed in the U.S.A.

ISBN 10:   0-54-725174-2
ISBN 13:   978-0-54-725174-5

123456789 0868 18 17 16 15 14 13 12 11 10 09

Hello, Reader!

Each day you are becoming a better reader. Good for you!

The stories in this book will take you to the sea, the jungle, and the desert. You will see animals that are furry, scaly, slinky, feathered, striped, and spotted. You will even read about sea slugs!

Get ready to read new words, visit new places, and learn about the world around us!

Sincerely,

The Authors

Nature Near and Far

Big Idea It's a big, wonderul world.

Nature
Near and Far

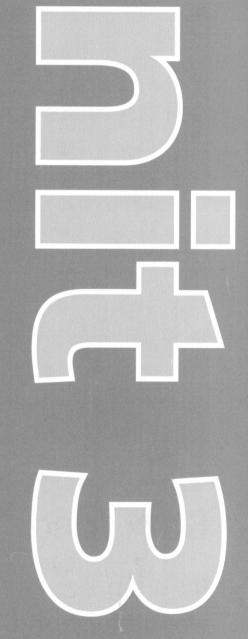

Unit 3

Big Idea

It's a big,
wonderful world.

Paired Selections

SEA ANIMALS
by Norbert Wu

Water

✔ WORDS TO KNOW
HIGH-FREQUENCY WORDS

cold
where
blue
live
far
their
little
water

Vocabulary
Reader

Shark
by Anita Sanders

Context
Cards

cold
This ocean water is
very cold.

cold
What Does It Mean?

Words to Know

Read
Together

● Read each Context Card.

● Make up a new sentence
that uses a blue word.

1

cold

This ocean water is
very cold.

2

where

Sharks live where the
ocean is deep.

3 blue

Today the ocean water looks blue.

4 live

Whales live in all the oceans of the world.

5 far

Squid swim far below the ocean's surface.

6 their

Their home is by the ocean.

7 little

Many little fish live in the ocean.

8 water

Some people take photos in the water.

Background

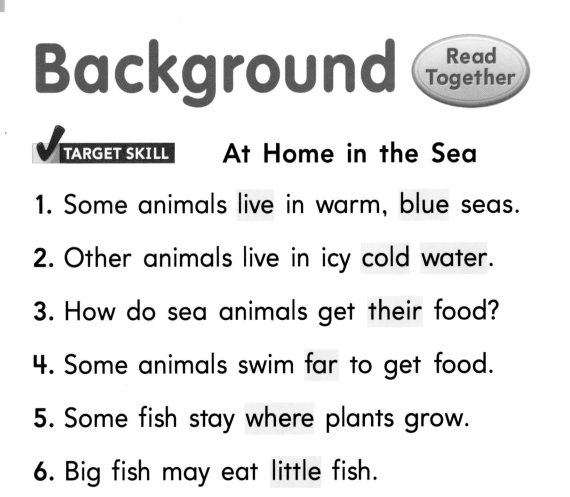

Read Together

✔ **TARGET SKILL**   **At Home in the Sea**

1. Some animals live in warm, blue seas.

2. Other animals live in icy cold water.

3. How do sea animals get their food?

4. Some animals swim far to get food.

5. Some fish stay where plants grow.

6. Big fish may eat little fish.

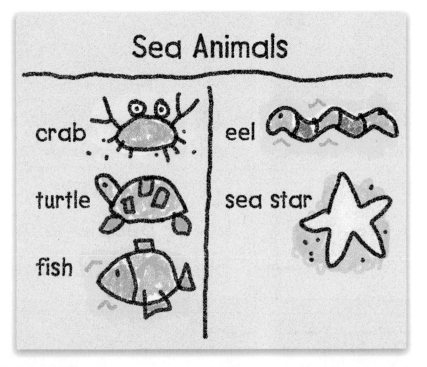

Name more big and little sea animals.

Comprehension

✓ **TARGET SKILL** Author's Purpose

Authors write for many reasons.
They write stories to make you laugh.
They write nonfiction
selections to give
information and help you
learn things. Good
readers think about why
an author writes.

As you read **Sea Animals**, figure out
why the author wrote and what he
wants to tell you.

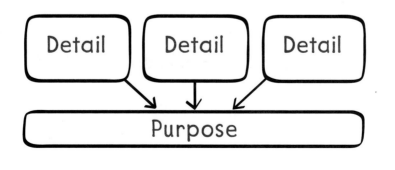

Main Selection

SEA ANIMALS
by Norbert Wu

✔ WORDS TO KNOW

cold	far
where	their
blue	little
live	water

✔ TARGET SKILL

Author's Purpose Tell why an author writes.

✔ TARGET STRATEGY

Analyze/Evaluate Tell how you feel about the text, and why.

GENRE

Informational text gives facts about a topic.

Meet the Author and Photographer

Norbert Wu

Norbert Wu's job as a nature photographer is exciting, but it can be dangerous. While taking photos of sea creatures, Mr. Wu has been attacked by sharks and trapped in an underwater cave. Check out his work in the book **Fish Faces**.

SEA ANIMALS

written and photographed by Norbert Wu

Essential Question

Why do authors write stories?

What is it like to live in the sea?

Lots of animals and plants live here.

giant jellyfish

The animals can be big.

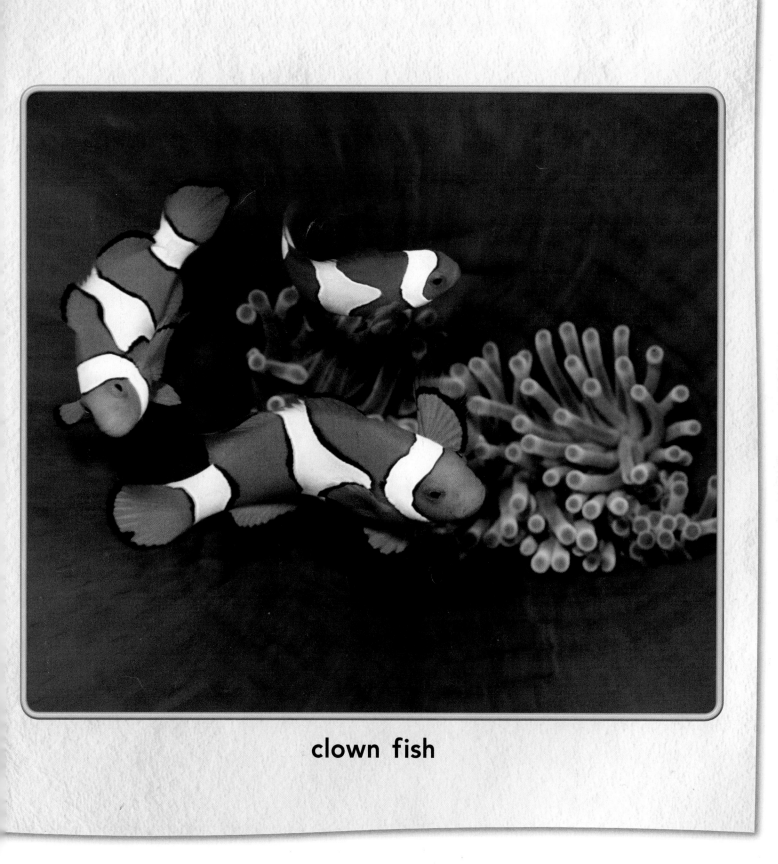

clown fish

They can be little.

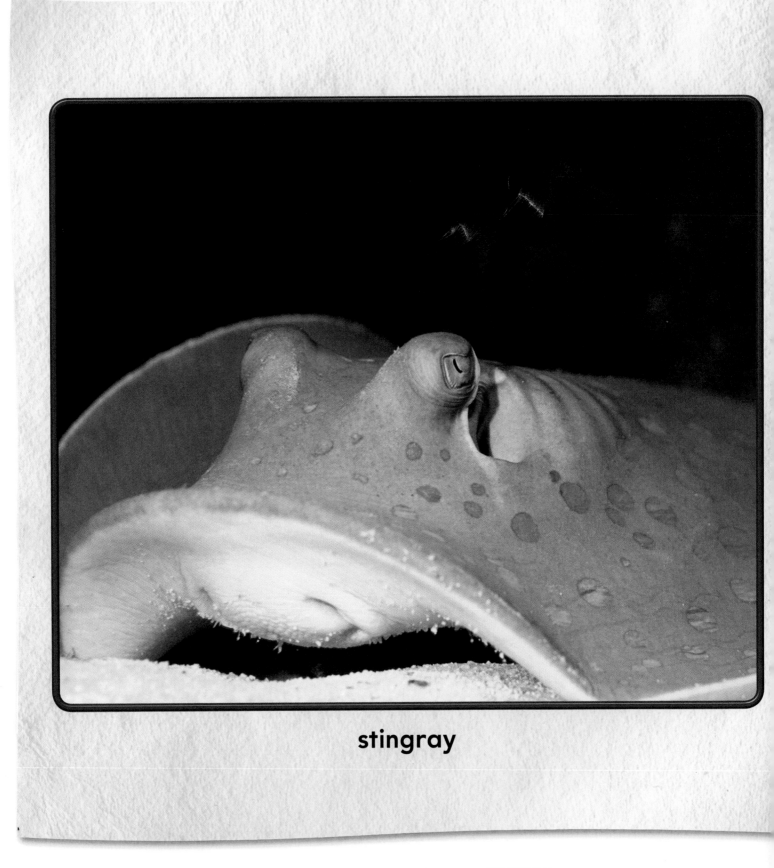

stingray

This flat fish has big blue spots.

ghost pipefish

This thin fish has pink spots.

sea slug

Some animals must be in water
to live. This sea slug can rest
on rocks in the water.

crab

Some animals can live in water and on land. This crab can run and dig in the sand.

penguins

Penguins can live where it is cold.
They just had a cold swim. Brrr!

California sea lions

Sea lions can live where it is warm.
They will nap on rocks in the sun.

A turtle is not fast on land.
It can swim fast in water.

It has flippers that help it swim fast. It can swim far.

sea star

Sea stars are not fast. They take little steps on sand and rocks.

moray eels

Some animals eat plants. Lots of them eat fish. Some will hunt for a snack with a pal.

The sea is full of lots of animals.
The water is their home.

Under the Sea

Create a Mural Make a sea mural with a partner. Work together to draw animals and plants that live in the sea. Look at the photographs in **Sea Animals** to help you.   PARTNERS

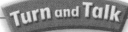 **Turn and Talk** — **Animal Facts**

Why do you think the author wrote **Sea Animals**? Talk about it with a partner. Then tell two facts you learned from the story.

AUTHOR'S PURPOSE

31

Water

What is one thing that all living things, whether they are big or little, have in common? They need water to live.

Water comes in different forms. The water you drink is a liquid. A liquid flows and takes the shape of the container it is in.

water

ice

snow

Water can freeze into ice or snow. Frozen water is a solid. A solid has its own shape.

What is ice? Ice is water that has frozen. It is hard and cold.

Where does snow come from? Snow is tiny pieces of frozen water that fall from the clouds.

Ice and snow are found in many places around the world. The North Pole is one of these places. There is cold, blue water all around it. People cannot live that far north for very long, but some animals make their homes near the North Pole.

Making Connections

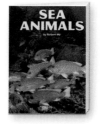

SEA ANIMALS

Water

📖 Text to Self

Write to Describe Think about your favorite sea animal from the selection. Write sentences to describe it to a classmate.

📖 Text to Text

Connect to Science Look at the pictures in **Sea Animals**. How many forms of water do you see? What are they?

🌐 Text to World

Use a Globe Use a globe to find two different oceans. Draw and label sea animals that you think might live in each ocean.

Grammar

Proper Nouns A noun that names a special person or animal is called a **proper noun**. Proper nouns begin with capital letters.

Nick Todd

Flipper

When a **title** is used before a name, it begins with a capital letter, too. A title usually ends with a period.

Mr. Diaz   **Mrs.** Sims   **Miss** Reed

Make up a name for each person and animal and write it on another sheet of paper. Use at least one title. Share your names with classmates.

1.
2.
3.
4.
5.

Grammar in Writing

When you proofread your writing, be sure you have written the names of people and animals correctly.

Write to Inform

✔ **Sentence Fluency** Sometimes you will write **sentences** that give readers facts. One kind of fact describes how something happens.

Joy wrote about sea lions. Then she added **loudly** to describe how sea lions bark.

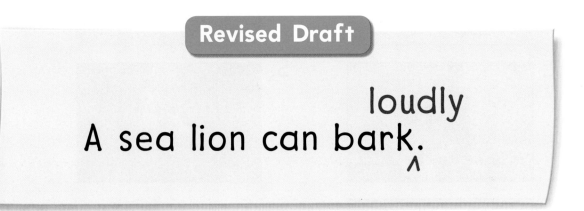

Revised Draft

loudly
A sea lion can bark.
                    ∧

Writing Traits Checklist

✔ **Sentence Fluency** Do my sentences have words that tell how?

✔ Did I spell words correctly?

✔ Did I use capital letters correctly?

38

Look for words that tell **how** in Joy's final copy. Then revise your writing. Use the Checklist.

Sea Lions

Sea lions do amazing things. A sea lion can bark loudly. It uses its flippers to move quickly on land or in water.

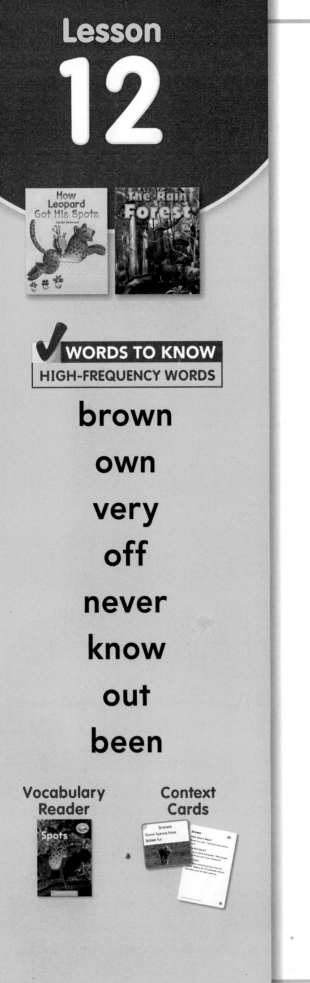

brown

own

very

off

never

know

out

been

Vocabulary
Reader

Context
Cards

Words to Know

● Read each Context Card.

● Describe a picture, using the blue word.

1

brown

Some hyenas have brown fur.

2

own

Zebras know their own mother by her stripes.

3 very

The snake in that tree is **very** long.

4 off

The bird flew **off** the rock and into the air.

5 never

Rhinos eat plants. They **never** eat meat.

6 know

Leopards **know** how to climb trees.

7 out

The turtle climbed **out** of the pond.

8 been

The giraffes have **been** moving fast.

Background

✓ **WORDS TO KNOW** **Animals with Spots**

1. You never know which spotted animals you might see when you go out.

2. There have been cows with very big spots.

3. Baby deer are brown with white spots.

4. Look at a ladybug's spots before it flies off.

5. Make your own list of animals with spots.

Some Animals with Spots

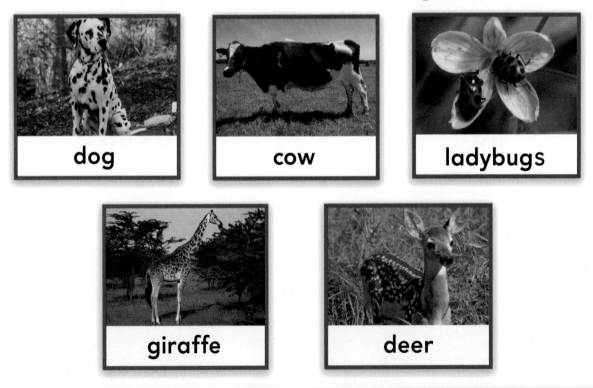

dog   cow   ladybugs

giraffe   deer

42

Comprehension

✔ **TARGET SKILL** Sequence of Events

Most story events are told in time order. This order is called the **sequence of events**. Good readers think about what happens **first, next,** and **last** so that a story makes sense. Tell about the sequence of events in this leopard's life.

As you read **How Leopard Got His Spots**, think about the sequence of events.

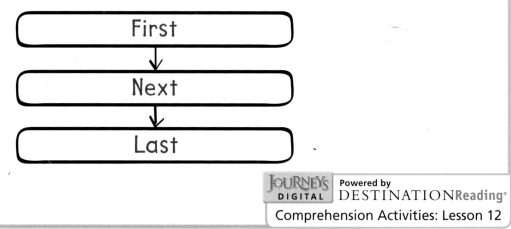

First
Next
Last

How Leopard Got His Spots
Gerald McDermott

✔ **WORDS TO KNOW**

brown	never
own	know
very	out
off	been

✔ **TARGET SKILL**

Sequence of Events
Tell the order in which things happen.

✔ **TARGET STRATEGY**

Question Ask questions about the story.

GENRE

A **folktale** is an old story people tell. Why is **once upon a time** used in this folktale?

Meet the Author and Illustrator

Gerald McDermott

When he was just four years old, Gerald McDermott started taking art lessons at a museum. Saturdays were spent at the museum drawing, painting, and looking at the artwork. Mr. McDermott's book **Arrow to the Sun** won the Caldecott Medal for best illustrations.

How Leopard Got His Spots

written and illustrated by Gerald McDermott

Essential Question

Why is the order of story events important?

Do you know how
Leopard got his spots?

Once upon a time, Fred
Turtle was playing catch with
Hal Hyena. Hal tricked Fred.
Then he ran away.

Fred felt very sad.
He called out for help.
"Help! I am stuck in
the plants," he yelled.

Len Leopard ran to help.

Chop! Chop! Chop!
Len cut the plants off and
let Fred out.

Fred and Len danced in the
sun.
"This is such fun!" they said.

"I have never been this glad,"
said Fred. "I like to paint if I
am glad!"

Fred mixed paints from many flowers. Then he painted black stripes on Zel Zebra.

Fred painted Jill Giraffe next.
"Look at me!" said Jill.
"I have big brown spots now."

54

"I like spots very much.
Can I have spots, too?"
asked Len.

Fred got set to paint Len.

Now Len had spots
of his very own.

Zel, Jill, and Len had such
fun looking at their spots
and stripes.
Hal said, "Paint me, too!"

But Fred had a trick for Hal.
He splashed Hal with brown
paint. Hal yelled and ran off.

Now Fred and Len
are best friends.

A New Friend

Write a Page Make a ne[w]
the story. Think of anoth[er]
that Fred might meet. [...]
to show how Fred woul[d]
friend. Write sentence[s]
your picture. PERSONA[L]

lizard
↓

Mix I[t]

Think of three thin[gs]
happened in the s[tory]
them to a partner [in]
wrong order. Hav[e your]
partner tell which [happened]
first, next, and las[t]
SEQUENCE OF EVENTS

toucan

jaguar

Forest Floor Sunlight almost never reaches this layer. Tapirs, jaguars, and beetles live on the brown forest floor. Ants and giant anteaters also live there. Anteaters have been known to eat thirty thousand insects in a single day!

NORTH AMERICA

EUROPE

ASIA

AFRICA

Equator

SOUTH AMERICA

AUSTRALIA

Map Key

Rain forest

ANTARCTICA

Do you know where the world's rain forests are? This map shows you.

sloth

eagle

monkey

toucan

jaguar

tapir

63

Forest Floor Sunlight almost never reaches this layer. Tapirs, jaguars, and beetles live on the brown forest floor. Ants and giant anteaters also live there. Anteaters have been known to eat thirty thousand insects in a single day!

NORTH AMERICA

EUROPE

ASIA

AFRICA

Equator

SOUTH AMERICA

AUSTRALIA

Map Key

Rain forest

ANTARCTICA

Do you know where the world's rain forests are? This map shows you.

Making Connections

Read Together

Text to Self

Write a Story What does **once upon a time** mean? Write a story about an animal you might see near your home. Begin your story with **once upon a time**.

Text to Text

Connect to Science Look back at both selections. Tell how the places where the animals live are alike and different.

Text to World

Make a Map Pretend that you are going to visit a rain forest. Draw a map showing where you will go. Explain any symbols you use on your map.

Grammar

Read Together

Proper Nouns A noun that names a special place is also a **proper noun**. Proper nouns begin with capital letters.

Turtle Park

Woods School

Vine Road

Spot Pond

Write each sentence correctly. Use another sheet of paper.

1. I go to the pratt school.

2. My class took a trip to the kent zoo.

3. It is on ash street in hampton.

4. Next year I am moving to texas.

5. My new house is near fisher lake.

Grammar in Writing

When you proofread your writing, be sure you have written the names of places correctly.

Write to Inform

✔ **Sentence Fluency** In good **instructions**, the sentences tell the steps in order. Order words help make the steps easy to follow.

Akil drafted his instructions in a letter to his friend Pam. Later, he added the order word **Last**.

Revised Draft

Last,
4. ~~C~~olor brown spots.
  ∧

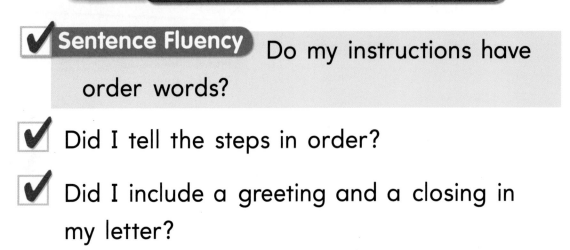

Writing Traits Checklist

✔ **Sentence Fluency** Do my instructions have order words?

✔ Did I tell the steps in order?

✔ Did I include a greeting and a closing in my letter?

68

Revise your work using the Checklist.
Follow Akil's instructions to make a puppet!

Final Copy

Dear Pam,

I made a leopard puppet. Here is how you can make one, too.

1. First, get a small paper bag.
2. Next, fold the sides of the flap.
3. Then, glue on ears, eyes, a nose, and whiskers.
4. Last, color brown spots.

I hope you have fun making your puppet.

    Your friend,

    Akil

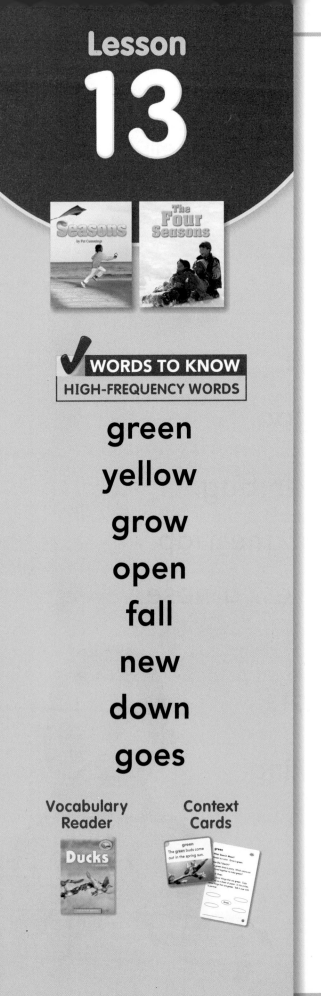

✓ **WORDS TO KNOW**
HIGH-FREQUENCY WORDS

green

yellow

grow

open

fall

new

down

goes

Vocabulary
Reader

Context
Cards

Words to Know

● **Read each Context Card.**

● **Choose two blue words.**
Use them in sentences.

1

green

The green buds come
out in the spring sun.

2

yellow

He put on yellow boots
on a rainy day.

3
grow
Many flowers grow in the summer.

4
open
The windows can be open on a hot day.

5
fall
The leaves change color in fall.

6
new
She has a brand new backpack for school.

7
down
Snow comes down on a cold day.

8
goes
She goes to the park to skate with her mom.

Background

Read Together

✓ **WORDS TO KNOW**   **Four Seasons**

1. Winter comes and goes.

2. A new season starts. It is spring!

3. Green plants grow. Then it is summer.

4. Many flowers are open in summer.

5. Fall comes next. Leaves turn yellow.

6. Snow falls down. Winter is here again.

Spring

Summer

Fall

Winter

Comprehension

✔ **TARGET SKILL**   Cause and Effect

One story event can make, or cause, another event to happen. The **cause** happens first. It is the reason why something else happens. The **effect** is what happens because of the first event.

Cause: It is raining.

Effect: The girls stand under an umbrella.

As you read **Seasons**, think about what happens in each season and why.

What happens?	Why?

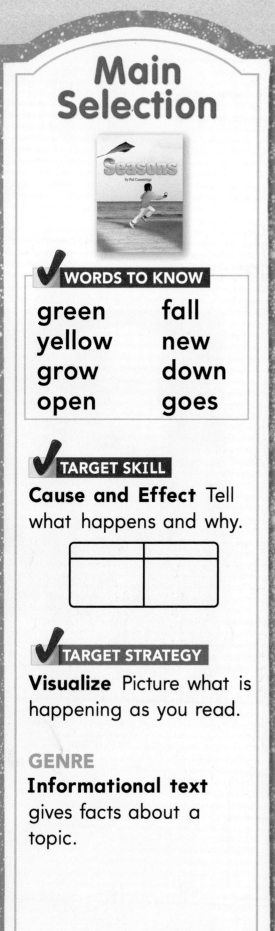

Seasons
by Pat Cummings

✔ **WORDS TO KNOW**

green	fall
yellow	new
grow	down
open	goes

✔ **TARGET SKILL**

Cause and Effect Tell what happens and why.

✔ **TARGET STRATEGY**

Visualize Picture what is happening as you read.

GENRE

Informational text gives facts about a topic.

Meet the Author

Pat Cummings

Pat Cummings loves getting letters from kids who have read her books. Sometimes they send her other things too, such as T-shirts, mugs, drawings, and even science projects. **Clean Your Room, Harvey Moon!** is just one of her many books.

Seasons

written by Pat Cummings

Essential Question

What changes do the different seasons cause?

Spring

In the spring,
fresh winds blow.
We plant new seeds,
and green buds grow.

Eggs hatch open.
Little chicks sing.
The sun is out.
It must be spring!

The grass gets wet.
Splish! Splash! Splish!
When we step,
we hear it squish.

Summer

Then summer is here
and it gets hot.
We are not in school.
We play a lot.

Bugs buzz and hum.
The plants grow tall.
Next to them,
I look small.

Summer goes fast,
and when it ends,
we will go back to school
with all our friends.

Fall

In fall the leaves
are red, yellow, and brown.
In a gust of wind,
they will fall down.

The leaves crunch
as we jump and hop.
It is such fun,
we cannot stop!

Animals get nuts
and pack them away.
They will have lots to eat
on a cold day.

Winter

When it is winter,
cold winds blow.
It is fun to sled
on the soft snow.

When it is cold,
some animals rest.
This animal has
a nap in a nest.

A hat on a shelf
gives us a plan.
We will put the hat
on a big snowman!

 **Winter**

 **Spring**

 **Summer**

 **Fall**

Winter, Spring,
Summer, Fall.
Which is best?
We like them all!

Your Turn

What's the Season?

Season Charades Work with a partner. Take turns acting out a season. Think of ways to show what the season is like. Be sure you do not use words! Have your partner guess which season you are. PARTNERS

Turn and Talk — What to Wear

What kinds of clothes do you wear in each season? Talk about it with a partner. Tell how the weather helps you decide what to wear. CAUSE AND EFFECT

Connect to Poetry

green	fall
yellow	new
grow	down
open	goes

GENRE

Poetry uses the sound of words to show pictures and feelings. Listen for rhythm and rhyme in the following poems.

TEXT FOCUS

Onomatopoeia is the use of words that imitate sounds.

The Four Seasons

The year goes by fast. Each season brings many changes. We see green grass grow each summer. In the fall, red and yellow leaves drift down from the trees. Snow comes in winter, and new flowers open up in spring.

Spring Song

The winter snow melts away
and the air is soft this sunny day.
What does this gentle wind sing?
I know! I know!
Here comes Spring!

by Charlotte Zolotow

Listen

Scrunch, scrunch, scrunch.
Crunch, crunch, crunch.
Frozen snow and brittle ice
Make a winter sound that's nice
Underneath my stamping feet
And the cars along the street.
Scrunch, scrunch, scrunch.
Crunch, crunch, crunch.

by Margaret Hillert

Seasons Song

to the tune of "Twinkle, Twinkle, Little Star"

Winter, spring, summer, fall,
Which one is the best of all?
Winter has the cold and snow.
Spring has rain so flowers grow.
Summer has the hot, hot sun.
Fall has school and friends and fun.

Write About the Seasons

Draw a picture of your favorite season. Then write a poem about it. Try using rhyming words and sound words.

Making Connections

Read Together

Text to Self

Write to Describe What is your favorite season? Write sentences to describe it.

Text to Text

Connect to Poetry List pairs of rhyming words from the selections. Choose a pair and write two more rhyming words.

Text to World

Tell About Seasons Locate your state on a globe. Then locate a country. Tell how you think the seasons in both places might be the same or different.

Grammar

Read Together

Subjects and Verbs In a sentence, the subject and the verb have to agree. Both must tell about the same number of people or things. Add **s** to most **verbs** when they tell about a **noun** that names one.

One	More Than One
One **boy pulls** his sled.	Two **girls pull** their dog.
Brett slides down the hill.	**Children slide** across the pond.

98

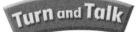

Choose the correct verb to finish each sentence. Take turns reading a sentence aloud with a partner. Then talk about how you chose the correct verb.

1. Raindrops _____?_____ each spring.
   fall   falls

2. Flowers _____?_____ in the garden.
   grow   grows

3. One bug _____?_____ all night.
   hum   hums

4. Now the sun _____?_____ brightly.
   shine   shines

5. The children _____?_____ in the pool.
   swim   swims

Grammar in Writing

When you proofread your writing, be sure you have written the correct verb to go with each noun.

Write to Inform

☑ Ideas When you write **sentences** that tell facts, be sure all your sentences are about one main idea.

Kyle wrote about winter. Then he took out a sentence that didn't belong.

Revised Draft

Winter is the coldest season.

Sometimes it snows here.

~~I have a sled.~~

Writing Traits Checklist

☑ Ideas Are all my sentences about one main idea?

☑ Does each detail sentence tell a fact?

☑ Did I write the correct verb to go with each noun?

Look for the main idea sentence in Kyle's final copy. Then revise your writing. Use the Checklist.

Final Copy

A Chilly Season

Winter is the coldest season.

Sometimes it snows here.

The lake freezes.

People skate on it.

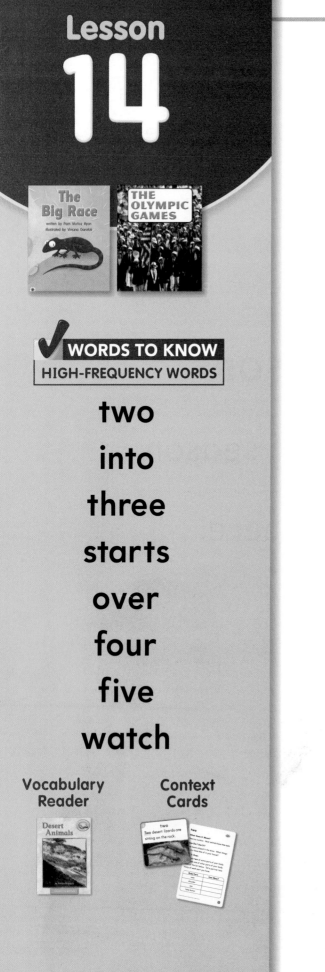

✔ **WORDS TO KNOW**
HIGH-FREQUENCY WORDS

two

into

three

starts

over

four

five

watch

Vocabulary
Reader

Context
Cards

Words to Know

Read Together

● **Read each** Context Card.

● **Use a blue word to tell about something you did.**

1
two
Two desert lizards are sitting on the rock.

2
into

The bird flew into the big cactus.

3 three

There are **three** birds resting in the sun.

4 starts

The desert **starts** to cool down at sunset.

5 over

A hawk flew **over** the tall rocks.

6 four

All **four** legs of this fox are strong.

7 five

This desert flower has **five** red spots.

8 watch

The rabbits **watch** and listen for danger.

Background

✓ **WORDS TO KNOW** **Running Contest**

1. The race starts at four o'clock.

2. We watch the runners get into place.

3. Five runners start to go fast.

4. Then three of the runners slow down.

5. Two runners are very close.

6. The winner goes over the finish line!

Who do you think will win this race?
Tell about races you have been in.

Comprehension

✔ **TARGET SKILL** Conclusions

In a story, authors do not always tell all the details. Readers must use story clues and what they already know to make a smart guess about what the author does not say. This smart guess is a **conclusion**.

Conclusion: The boy won.
What clues helped you know this?

As you read **The Big Race**, use story clues and what you already know to think of conclusions. Use a chart like this one to tell what helps Red Lizard win the race.

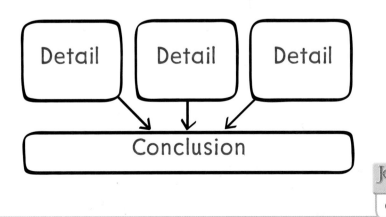

The Big Race
written by Pam Muñoz Ryan
illustrated by Viviana Garofoli

✓ **WORDS TO KNOW**

two	over
into	four
three	five
starts	watch

✓ **TARGET SKILL**

Conclusions Use details to figure out more about the text.

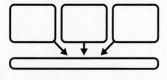

✓ **TARGET STRATEGY**

Infer/Predict Use clues to figure out more about story parts.

GENRE

A **fantasy** is a story that could not happen in real life.

Meet the Author

Pam Muñoz Ryan

California summers can be very hot. When Pam Muñoz Ryan was growing up, she was often at the library on summer days. That's because the library was one of the few places nearby with air conditioning!

Meet the Illustrator

Viviana Garofoli

Viviana Garofoli and her family make their home in the country of Argentina. **Sophie's Trophy** and **My Big Rig** are two of the books she has illustrated.

The Big Race

written by Pam Muñoz Ryan

illustrated by Viviana Garofoli

Essential Question

What clues help you figure out why events happen?

Win the Big Race
Win this Big Cake

Today is the big race.

"I like cake!" said Red Lizard.
"I will run in that race."

Red Lizard gets to the race.
Four animals will run with him.

Cottontail is not late.

She will run in lane one.

Rat naps in the shade.

She will run in lane two.

Snake takes his spot in lane three.

Roadrunner stands in lane four.

He waves to his pals.

Red Lizard is in lane five.

The animals bend and hop.

Get set.

Go!

The flag is down, and the race starts!
Many animals watch and clap.

Cottontail does not get far.

Rat falls into the hay.

Snake stops and chases bugs.

Roadrunner trips over a rake.

Who will win?

It's Red Lizard who wins!

"Watch me eat this cake," he yells.
Red Lizard looks at his big cake.

Red Lizard looks at his pals.

His pals like cake, too.
What will Red Lizard do now?

Red Lizard gets five plates.

He gets cake for his pals, too.

Hip, Hip, Hooray for Red Lizard!

Hip, Hip, Hooray!

Write Sentences Red Lizard cheers when he wins the big race. Write about something that made you cheer. What happened? How did you feel? PERSONAL RESPONSE

Turn and Talk — Figure It Out

Look at the end of the story. Why do you think Red Lizard shares the cake with his pals? Talk about it with a partner. Tell how the words and the pictures helped you decide. CONCLUSIONS

Connect to Social Studies

✔ **WORDS TO KNOW**

two	over
into	four
three	five
starts	watch

GENRE

Informational text gives facts about a topic. This is a magazine article.

TEXT FOCUS

Captions tell more information about a photo or picture. Read captions to find facts.

THE OLYMPIC GAMES

by Margaret Bishop

The Olympic Games are sports games. Athletes come from many countries to play. Many people watch, too. Here are three American athletes who have been in the Olympics.

A parade starts the Olympic Games.

Lake Placid, New York, 1980

Eric Heiden was a speed skater. He was in five races, and he won all of them! He skated into history.

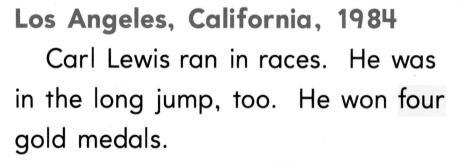

Los Angeles, California, 1984

Carl Lewis ran in races. He was in the long jump, too. He won four gold medals.

Carl won nine gold medals in four different Olympics.

Atlanta, Georgia, 1996

Kerri Strug had two tries to go over the vault. She fell once, but she tried again. She did it!

Making Connections

Text to Self

Write About Sports Which sport would you like to win? Draw yourself winning. Write a sentence to go with it. Capitalize the first word.

Text to Text

Connect to Social Studies Think about the selections. Discuss with a partner which one is real and which is fantasy. Take turns and tell how you know.

Text to World

Map a Race Course Pretend you will run a race through your neighborhood. Where does the race begin? Where is the finish line? Draw a race course map.

Grammar

Read Together

Verbs and Time Some **verbs** tell what is happening now. Some verbs tell what happened in the past. Add **ed** to most verbs to tell about the past.

Now	In the Past
The **animals watch** the race now.	The **animals watched** the race yesterday.
They cheer for their friends.	**They cheered** for their friends.

130

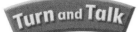

Work with a partner. One partner reads aloud a sentence. The other partner finds the verb. Together, tell how to write the verb to tell about the past. Take turns.

1. The runners look at the flag.

2. They start the race.

3. Some racers jump high.

4. They finish the race quickly.

5. The winners pick prizes.

Grammar in Writing

When you proofread your writing, be sure each verb tells clearly if something is happening now or in the past.

Write to Inform

Read Together

✓ **Ideas** A good **report** needs facts!
Before you start writing, find facts to answer
the question you wrote about your topic.

Lena found information about lizards.
She took notes to remind her of the facts.

Exploring a Topic

Prewriting Checklist

✓ Did I write a good question about my topic?

✓ Will my notes help me remember the facts?

✓ Did I use good sources for information?

Look for facts in Lena's notes. Then record your own notes. Use the Checklist.

Planning Chart

My Question
What do real lizards do?

Fact 1
change color

Fact 2
run fast on back legs

Fact 3
puff up to look big

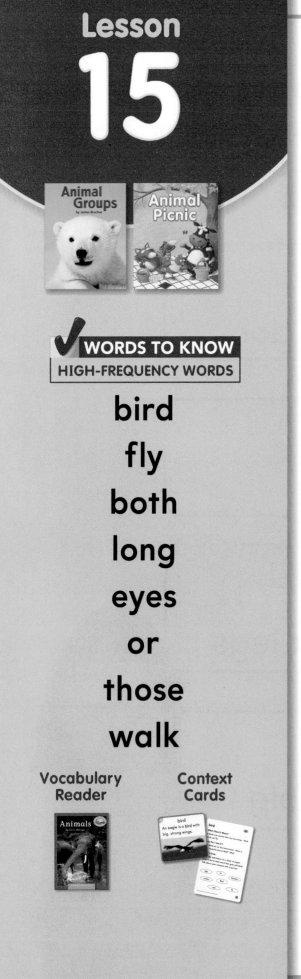

Animal Groups
by James Bruchac

Animal Picnic

✓ WORDS TO KNOW
HIGH-FREQUENCY WORDS

bird

fly

both

long

eyes

or

those

walk

Vocabulary Reader   Context Cards

Animals

Words to Know

- Read each Context Card.

- Ask a question that uses one of the blue words.

1

bird

An eagle is a bird with big, strong wings.

2

fly

Bats are mammals that are able to fly.

3 both
The lizard has both stripes and spots.

4 long
This kangaroo has a long tail.

5 eyes
This dog has blue eyes.

6 or
Ducks can either swim or fly.

7 those
Those fish are not the same colors.

8 walk
The elephants walk together in a group.

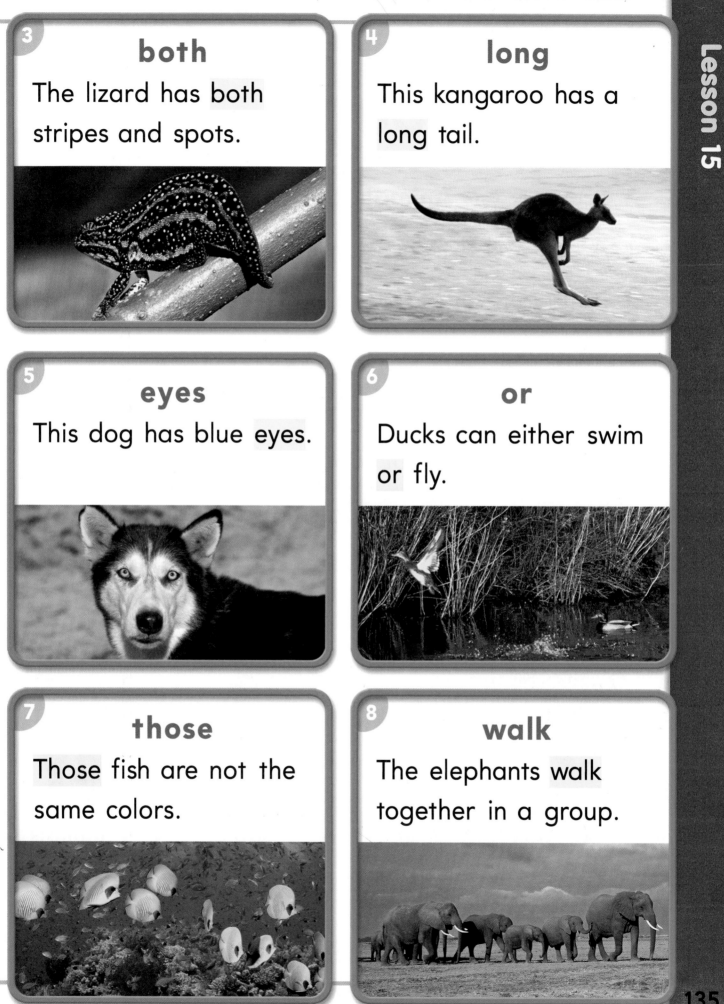

Background

Read Together

✓ **WORDS TO KNOW** Animals on the Move

1. A bird will fly, and a fish will swim.

2. Both lions and foxes run.

3. Frogs hop or swim.

4. A giraffe will walk on long legs.

5. A hawk's eyes spot food, and it dives.

6. Those are some ways animals move.

Four Animal Groups

| Reptiles | Fish | Birds | Mammals |

Can you name these animals?

Name more animals in each group.

Comprehension

Read Together

✔ **TARGET SKILL**   Compare and Contrast

When you **compare**, tell how things are the same. When you **contrast**, tell how things are different. Good readers think of how things are alike and different to help them understand a story better. How are a dog and a cat alike? How are they different?

As you read **Animal Groups**, think about the ways animals from different groups are the same and different.

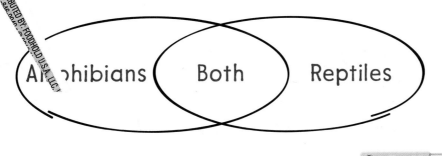

Amphibians   Both   Reptiles

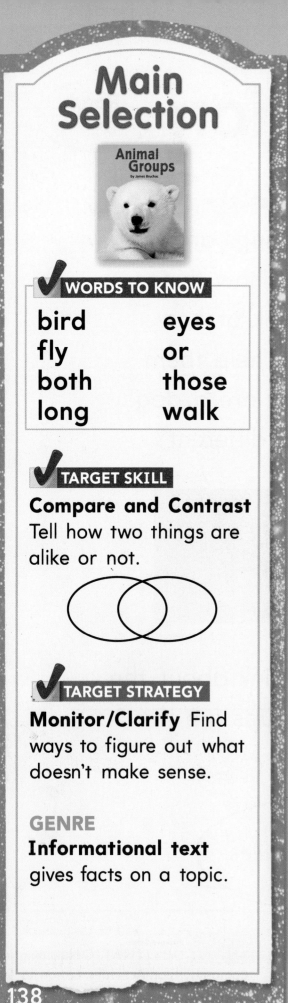

✔ **WORDS TO KNOW**

bird	eyes
fly	or
both	those
long	walk

✔ **TARGET SKILL**

Compare and Contrast
Tell how two things are alike or not.

✔ **TARGET STRATEGY**

Monitor/Clarify Find ways to figure out what doesn't make sense.

GENRE
Informational text gives facts on a topic.

Meet the Author

James Bruchac

James Bruchac has many interests. He is a writer, a storyteller, an animal tracker, and a wilderness guide. Together with his father, Joseph Bruchac, he wrote the books **How Chipmunk Got His Stripes** and **Turtle's Race with Beaver**.

Animal Groups

written by James Bruchac

Essential Question

How are animals the same and different?

Fish

Amphibian

Reptile

Let's take a look at five animal groups.

Bird

Mammal

How are animals in a group the same?

Fish

fin

eye

mouth

gill

fin

Fish must live in water. Fish have gills
that help them breathe in water.

tail

Fish have fins and tails. Those help them swim.

Fish can be many shapes and sizes.
Can you find a fish in this picture?

Reptiles

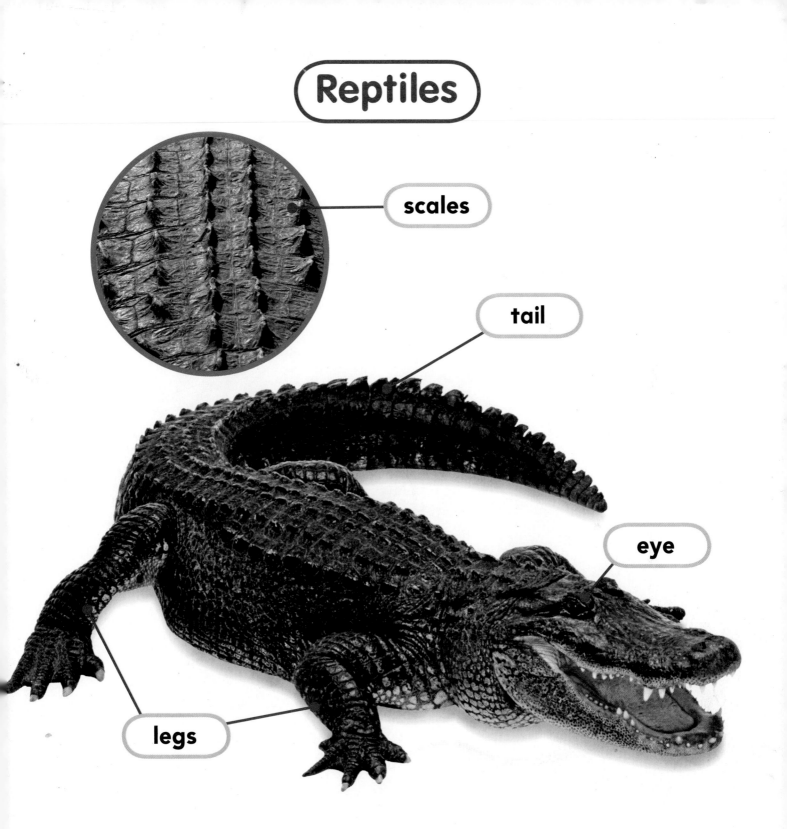

scales

tail

eye

legs

Reptiles can live on land. Some like to be in water. Reptiles have scales on their skin.

Many reptiles hatch from eggs.

Snakes cannot walk. They do not have legs. This snake slides its long body on the grass.

Amphibians

eye

wet skin

legs

Amphibians spend time both on land
and in water. They do not have scales.
Their skin is wet.

tadpoles

Amphibians hatch from eggs.
Tadpoles hatch and grow to be frogs.

Birds

eye

bill

wing

feathers

A bird has feathers and wings. This
bird's eyes are on the sides of its face!

Many birds can fly. Some can run
or swim fast.

Birds hatch from eggs. This
hen made a nest for its eggs.

Mammals

eye

hair

tail

legs

Mammals can be many shapes and sizes.

They have hair on their skin.

A mammal mom can
make milk for its baby.

Lots of mammals live on land,
but some live in water.

Did you know that you are a mammal, too?

Your Turn

Guess the Group!

Write a Riddle   Write a riddle about one of the animal groups in the story.   Read your riddle to a partner.   Have your partner guess the animal group.   PARTNERS

I have gills and live in water.

Turn and Talk — Alike and Different

Work with a partner. Choose two animals that are shown in **Animal Groups**. Make sure the animals are from different groups. Talk about how they are alike and different.

COMPARE AND CONTRAST

Connect to Plays

✔ **WORDS TO KNOW**

bird	eyes
fly	or
both	those
long	walk

GENRE

A **play** is a story that people act out.

TEXT FOCUS

Stage directions in plays tell about the characters and setting.

Animal Picnic

by Debbie O'Brien

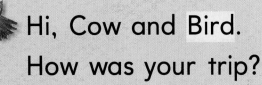

Cast of Characters

Fox

Cow

Bird

 Hi, Cow and Bird. How was your trip?

 I had to **walk** to get here.

I had to **fly**.

(pointing to Cow's basket)
What food did you bring for our picnic?

I brought grass. I use my flat teeth to grind it.

 I brought meat. I use my long, sharp teeth to eat it.

We both have teeth, but we eat different things!

(pointing to Bird's basket)
What did you bring, Bird?

159

I did not bring grass or meat.
I brought seeds. Birds don't
have any teeth!

How will you eat those seeds
without teeth?

 Keep your eyes on me!
(Bird eats some seeds.)
Yum, yum, yum!

Making Connections

Text to Self

Talk About Animals Which animal group is your favorite? Discuss with a partner.

Text to Text

Connect to Language Arts Choose an animal from **Animal Groups**. Then think about the play. Write what that animal might say and do at the picnic.

Text to World

List Questions Think of an animal you would like to know more about. List questions you have about the animal. Where could you find the answers?

Grammar

Read Together

The Verb be The verbs **is** and **are** tell what is happening now. Use **is** with a noun that names one.

One	More Than One
This **chick is** small.	Two **chicks are** small.

The verbs **was** and **were** tell what happened in the past. Use **was** with a noun that names one.

One	More Than One
One **egg was** here.	Two **eggs were** here.

162

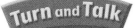

Read each sentence aloud two times, saying a different verb each time. Ask your partner to repeat the sentence with the correct verb. Then switch roles.

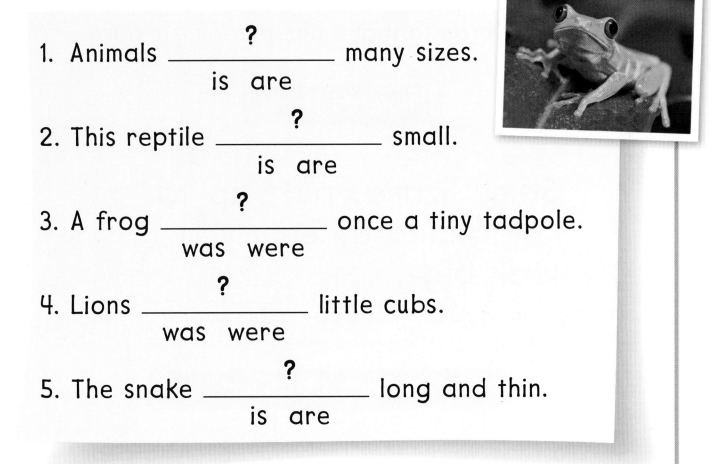

1. Animals ___**?**___ many sizes.
   is are

2. This reptile ___**?**___ small.
   is are

3. A frog ___**?**___ once a tiny tadpole.
   was were

4. Lions ___**?**___ little cubs.
   was were

5. The snake ___**?**___ long and thin.
   is are

Grammar in Writing

When you proofread your writing, be sure you have used the verbs **is**, **are**, **was**, and **were** correctly.

Write to Inform

☑ **Word Choice** In a good **report**, the right words make the facts easy to understand.

Lena drafted her report. Later, she wrote different words to make her meaning clear.

Revised Draft

with air
Some lizards puff up ∧ to
bigger to an enemy ∧
look ~~big~~.

 Revising Checklist

✔ Did I use words that make my meaning clear?

✔ Did I use correct punctuation?

✔ Did I spell words correctly?

Look for exact words in Lena's final copy. Then revise your writing. Use the Checklist.

An Interesting Reptile

Lizards do some funny things.

Some can change color quickly.

Others run fast using only their

back legs. Some lizards

puff up with air to look

bigger to an enemy.

Read
Together

Read the next two selections. Then tell what the authors want you to learn.

Frogs and Toads

Frogs and toads are alike in some ways. They both lay eggs in water. They both live in water when they are small. They both eat lots of bugs.

Frogs and toads are different in some ways, too. Frogs have smooth, wet skin. Frogs live in or near water. They have long back legs, too. This helps them hop and swim.

Toads have dry, bumpy skin. Toads spend much of their time on land. They have small back legs. This helps them walk.

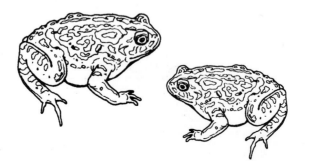

Roly-Poly Bugs

A pill bug is also called a roly-poly. It is a very small animal. It can roll into a little ball that looks like a pill. This helps to keep it safe from danger.

Pill bugs hatch from eggs. They like to live in places that are damp. Many pill bugs live under leaves, rocks, or logs.

Many people think pill bugs are insects. They are not. Insects have six legs, but a pill bug has fourteen legs. It is in the same animal group as a crab!

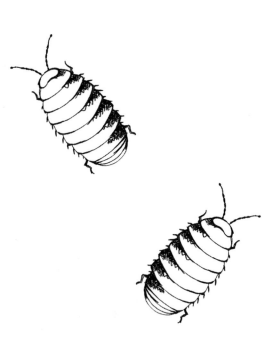

Unit 3 Wrap-Up

The Big Idea

Animal Wonders Think about the animals from the stories you have read. Write three things you learned about the ways animals live.

sea turtle

Sea turtles walk slow, but they can swim fast.

Listening and Speaking

Who Am I? Play an animal guessing game with a small group. Take turns acting out different animals, such as sea lion, elephant, or roadrunner. Others try to guess the animal.

168

Words to Know

Unit 3   High-Frequency Words

⑪ Sea Animals

cold	far
where	their
blue	little
live	water

⑭ The Big Race

two	over
into	four
three	five
starts	watch

⑫ How Leopard Got His Spots

brown	never
own	know
very	out
off	been

⑮ Animal Groups

bird	eyes
fly	or
both	those
long	walk

⑬ Seasons

green	fall
yellow	new
grow	down
open	goes

Glossary

A

amphibians

An **amphibian** is an animal that lives in water and on land. Frogs are **amphibians**.

B

blow

To **blow** means to push air. The winds **blow** the cold air across the land.

body

The **body** of a person or animal is made up of the parts you can see and touch. We are learning about the parts of the **body**.

breathe

To **breathe** is to take in breaths of air. I **breathe** in the fresh air when I am outside.

C

cottontail

A **cottontail** is a kind of rabbit. That **cottontail** has a white fluffy tail.

D

danced

To **dance** means to move to music. We played music and **danced** for hours.

day

A **day** is the time from one morning to the next morning. Tuesday was a sunny **day**.

F

feathers

A **feather** is a part of a bird. The bird had soft feathers.

fish

A **fish** is an animal that lives in water. My uncle has a yellow **fish** with black stripes.

flippers

A **flipper** is a kind of arm that helps an animal swim. The seal used its **flippers** to move in the water.

flowers

A **flower** is a part of a plant. We planted pretty **flowers** in the garden.

G

giraffe

A **giraffe** is a tall spotted animal with a long neck. The **giraffe** ate leaves from the top of the tree.

group

A **group** is a number of people or things together. A **group** of us went swimming last Saturday.

H

hair

Hair is what grows on your head. My dad cuts my **hair** when it gets too long.

hay

Hay is a kind of grass that has been cut and dried. My horse likes to eat **hay**.

home

A **home** is a place where people or animals live. Jellyfish make their **home** underwater.

hooray

Hooray is something people shout when they are happy. When I hit a home run, my parents yelled **hooray!**

hyena

A **hyena** is a wild animal that looks like a dog. The **hyena** is found in Africa and Asia.

L

leaves

A **leaf** is a part of a plant. In the fall, the **leaves** turn pretty colors.

leopard

A **leopard** is a wild animal that looks like a cat with spots. The **leopard** paced in its cage.

lions

A **lion** is a large wild animal that looks like a big cat. We saw a movie about **lions** in Africa.

lizard

A **lizard** is a small reptile. The **lizard** lay on the rock in the hot sun.

M

mammals

A **mammal** is a warm-blooded animal.
Cats are **mammals**.

P

paints

To **paint** means to cover something with color. My Aunt Carly **paints** houses.

penguins

A **penguin** is a kind of bird that lives in cold places. **Penguins** keep their chicks warm.

pink

Pink is a very light shade of red. My sister painted her nails **pink**.

R

race

A **race** is a contest to find out who is the fastest. Selena got to the finish line first and won the **race**.

reptiles

A **reptile** is a cold-blooded animal. Snakes are **reptiles**.

roadrunner

A **roadrunner** is a very fast bird. We saw a **roadrunner** in the Arizona desert.

S

school

A **school** is a place where students learn from teachers. My best friend and I go to the same **school**.

sea

A **sea** is a big body of water. The **sea** is filled with all kinds of fish.

sea lions

A **sea lion** is a large seal that lives by the ocean. **Sea lions** swim and then rest up on the rocks.

sea stars

A **sea star** is an ocean animal with long arms and thick skin. **Sea stars** are also called <u>starfish</u>.

seeds

A **seed** is a part of a plant. Most plants grow from tiny little **seeds**.

snow

Snow is tiny pieces of frozen water that fall from the clouds. When we woke up, the ground was covered with **snow**.

snowman

A **snowman** looks like a person made of snow. We piled three balls of snow on top of each other and made a **snowman**.

spring

Spring is the season that comes after winter. In the **spring,** the flowers begin to bloom.

summer

Summer is the season that comes after spring. This **summer** my family will go to the beach.

T

tadpoles

A **tadpole** is a baby frog. I found **tadpoles** swimming in our pond.

tails

A **tail** is a part of some animals' bodies. Rats have long **tails**.

tall

To be **tall** is to stand high above the ground. The giraffe is very **tall**.

turtle

A **turtle** is a reptile with a shell. The **turtle** went inside its shell as soon as I touched it.

W

warm

Warm means not very hot. The tea was still **warm** after it sat for a while.

wings

A **wing** is a part that helps something to fly. The bird flapped its **wings** and flew away.

winter

Winter is a season that comes after fall. Last **winter** was very cold!

Z

zebra

A **zebra** is a striped animal that looks like a horse. My favorite animal is the **zebra**.

Acknowledgments

"Listen" by Margaret Hillert. Reprinted by permission of the author who controls all rights.

"Spring Song" from *Seasons: A Book of Poems* by Charlotte Zolotow. Copyright © 2002 by Charlotte Zolotow. Reprinted by permission of HarperCollins Publishers.

Credits

Photo Credits

Placement Key: (t) top; (b) bottom; (l) left; (r) right; (c) center; (bkgd) background; (frgd) foreground; (i) inset.
TOC **8a** (c) (c)Alaska Stock LLC/Alamy; TOC **8b** Spread (c)age fotostock/SuperStock; **9** (tc) (c)Alaska Stock LLC/Alamy; **10** (t) (c)Konrad Wothe/Minden Pictures; **10** (b) (c)Reinhard Dirscherl/AGE FotoStock; **11** (tl) (c)Amanda Friedman/Stone/Getty Images; (tr) (c)Ron Sanford/Corbis; (cl) (c)George Grall/National Geographic/Getty Images; (cr) (c)Stockbyte; (bl) (c)Getty; (br) (c)Purestock/Getty Images; **12** HMCo; **14-30** (c)Norbert Wu Productions; **32** (c) (c)Lew Robertson/Getty Images; **41** (bg) (c) Siede Preis; **33** (bg) (c)Photodisc/Cybermedia; **35** inset (c)Andres Stapff/Reuters/Corbis; **36** (c) (c)George Grail/Getty Images; **37** (tl) (c) Johnny Johnson/Getty Images; (cl) (c)Vittorio Sciosia/Alamy; (bl) (c)Roger Tidman/CORBIS; (tr) (c)Jose B. Ruiz/naturepl.com; (cr) (c)Robert Brenner/PhotoEdit; **39** (br) HMCO; **40** (t) (c) Photodisc; **40** (b) (c) 1997 PhotoDisc, Inc. All rights reserved. Images provided by (c) 1997 Alan D. Carey; **41** (tl) (c)Design Pics Inc./Alamy; (tr) (c)Roger Tidman/CORBIS; (cl) (c)Ann & Steve Toon/Robert Harding World Imagery/Getty Images ; (cr) (c)Gallo Images/Alamy; (bl) (c)Rainer Jahns/Alamy; (br) (c)Tom Nebbia/CORBIS; **42** (tl) (tc) (tr) (br) Corel Stock Photo Library; **42** (bl) Corbis; **65-66** (c)Tony Craddock/Photo Researchers, Inc.; **67** (c)Wayne Barret/CORBIS; **69** Hmco; **70** (t) (c)Andrew Duke/Alamy; **70** (b) (c)Stock Connection Distribution/Alamy; **71** (tl) (c)Darrell Gulin/Corbis; (tr) (c)Jean Louis Bellurget/Stock Image/Jupiterimages; (cl) (c)Pete Turner/The Image Bank/Getty Images; (cr) (c) Ryan McVay/Taxi/Getty Images; (bl) (c)VEER Gildo Spadoni/Photonica/Getty Images; (br) (c) Steve Mason/PhotoDisc/Getty Images; **72** (c) Willy Matheisl/Alamy; **73** (c)Richard Hutchings/ Photo Edit; **74** (inset) (c)Courtesy of Pat